# Easter egg

## STICKER ACTIVITY FUN BOOK

D1332159

Have fun with this activity book!

Use your pencils and stickers to finish
the activities on each page. Where there is a
missing sticker, you will see this pattern:

There are cool door hangers and an Easter basket
to press out and decorate, too!

make
believe
ideas

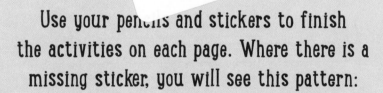

# EASTER EGG HUNT

Can you spot and circle Bunny's favourite three eggs on the page below?

1.

2.

3.

Sticker Bunny's eggs.
Then circle your
favourite egg.

Sticker the
missing eggs
to complete
the pattern.

# JELLY BEAN JUMBLE

Count how many coloured beans are inside the sweet jar.

pink beans  ..........

blue beans ..........

yellow beans ..........

red beans ..........

green beans ..........

Colour the Easter basket using your best pens and pencils.

# BEAUTIFUL BUNTING

## Use stickers to complete the patterns in each row.

Design your own bunting, too!

# SWEET SEARCH

Find all five words in the wordsearch. Words can go down or across.

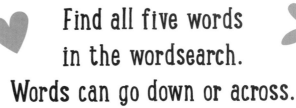

basket

~~bunny~~

~~chocolate~~

~~egg~~

~~treats~~

```
b s t r b
g k u r r b
y x n t e q j
n r j n h a z d h
s n m y r t y s t n
k b f j r s r t n
c h o c o l a t e
t s h x j r j n g
l n r d k t c h g
b a s k e t k
z r i c r
```

5

# STICKER BY NUMBERS

Use the key to sticker the Easter eggs and discover beautiful patterns.

Fill in the eggs with colour.

KEY: 1 = 2 = 3 =
4 = 5 = 6 =

# PERFECT PAIRS

Draw lines to match the
Easter egg pairs.

# EASTER EGG MAZE

Guide the bunny through the maze
to find some yummy Easter treats.

Start

Finish

Find the missing stickers along the way.

8

# SPOT THE DIFFERENCE

The animals are having an Easter party.

Circle seven differences between the scenes.

9

# TREAT TROUBLE

Bella the bunny has lost some of her Easter treats. Can you help her find them?

How many of each item can you find in the picture?

cupcakes  ( .............. )

strawberries  ( .............. )

Easter eggs  ( .............. )

chocolate bars  ( .............. )

carrots  ( .............. )

# EGG-CELLENT EGGS

Look at the rows of Easter eggs,
then use your stickers to fill in the answers.

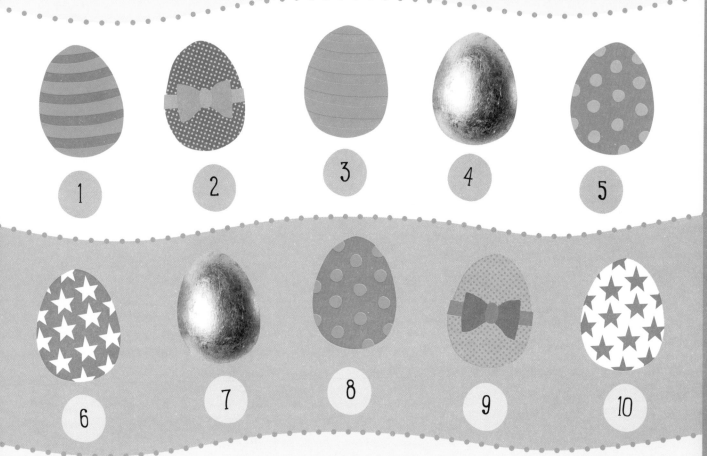

Which Easter egg is
pink with orange dots?

**5**

Which Easter egg has blue
and green stripes?

Which Easter egg
is white with pink stars?

Which Easter egg
wears an orange bow?

Which Easter egg
has a gold wrapper?

# BUNNY'S BONNET

Draw the missing half of the bonnet. Use the grid to help you.

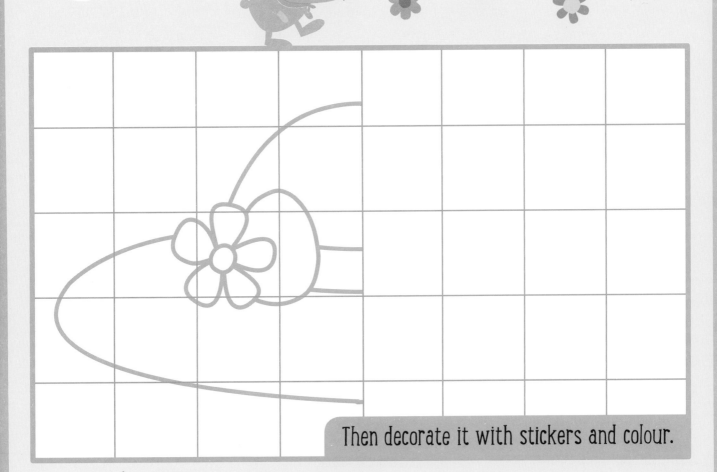

Then decorate it with stickers and colour.

Use your pencils to colour the flowers.

# SWEET COUNT

Find the missing stickers.
Then help the chicks finish their sums.

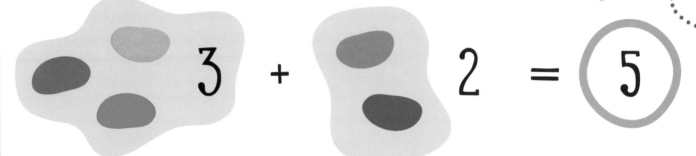

$3 + 2 = 5$

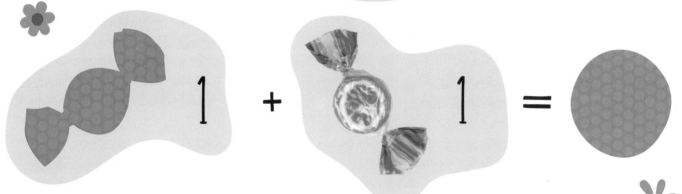

$1 + 1 = $

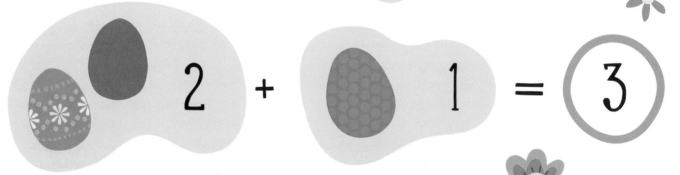

$2 + 1 = 3$

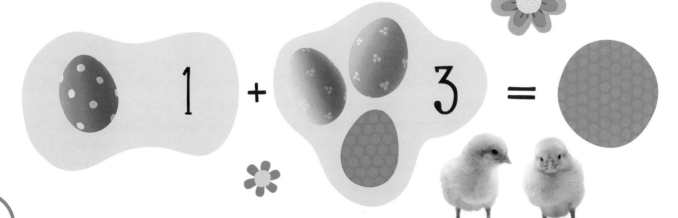

$1 + 3 = $

# FUNNY FACES

Draw and sticker funny faces on the eggs.

How many lollipops can you see?

..........

# EASTER PARADE

Help the animals put on a parade.
Lead them along the right path
using the key below.

|  |  |  |  |
|---|---|---|---|
| ↑ | → | ↓ | ← |

**Start**

**Finish**

# BUNNY'S BEDROOM

Press out and decorate the door hangers using your stickers.
Then, place them on your door handle for everyone to see!

EASTER BUNNY,
please stop here!

I'm not in right now,
I'm busy hunting
for EASTER EGGS!

# BUNNY BASKET

Ask an adult to help you make your basket.

Tape here

Tape here

## INSTRUCTIONS:

Press out the basket piece and curl it around to make a cone shape. Tape this edge to the inside of the cone.

Tape here

Next, press out the basket handle and bend it into a curved shape. Carefully tape one end to the inside of the basket, then tape the other end to the opposite side.

Finally, glue the ears, eyes, and mouth. Stick these on the front of your basket, and enjoy collecting your Easter treats!

Tape here

HANDLE

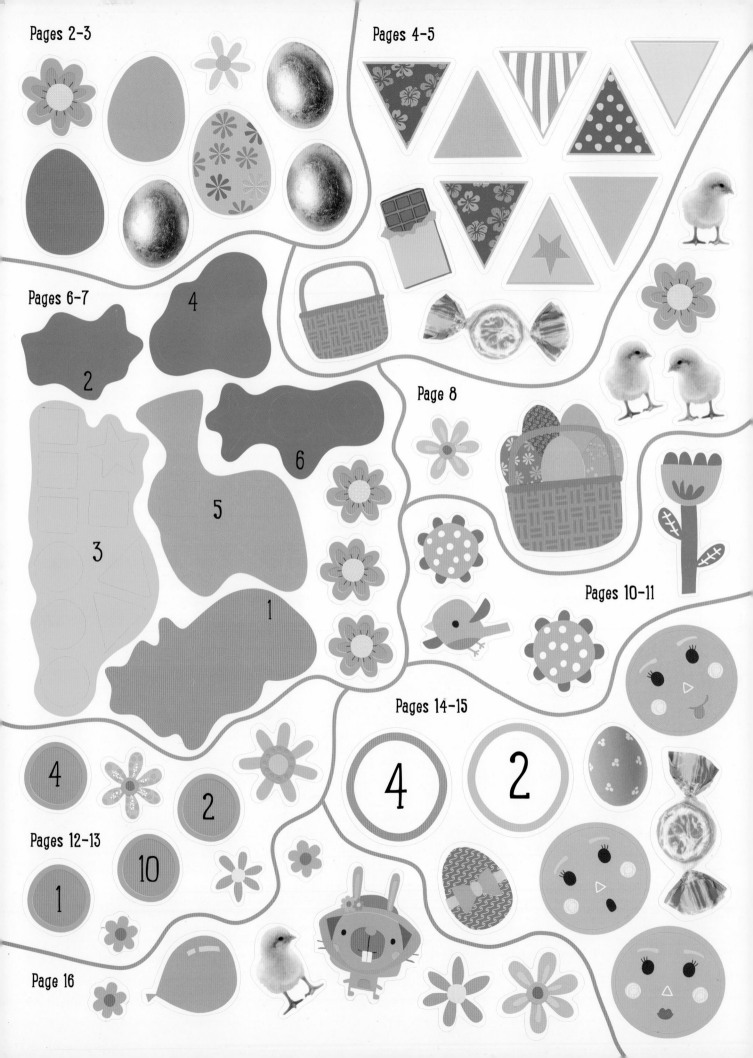

Pages 2-3

Pages 4-5

Pages 6-7

Page 8

Pages 10-11

Pages 14-15

Pages 12-13

Page 16

Extra stickers